COMMERCIAL REAL ESTATE INVESTING

A guide to creating a passive income and developing wealth.

Vicky Collier

All rights reserved. No part of this publication may be reproduced, distributed, or transmitted in any form or by any means, including photocopying, recording, or other electronic or mechanical methods, without the prior written permission of the publisher, except in the case of brief quotations embodied in critical reviews and certain other noncommercial uses permitted by copyright law.

Copyright © Vicky Collier, 2022.

Table of contents

Chapter 1

Chapter 2

Chapter 3

Chapter 4

Chapter 1

Commercial real estate (CRE) is property used entirely for business-related reasons or to offer a work area rather than a dwelling space, which would instead constitute residential real estate. Most typically, commercial real estate is leased to tenants to undertake income-generating operations. This vast category of real estate may contain anything from a single storefront to a big retail mall.

Commercial real estate comes in several ways. It may be anything from an office building to a residential duplex, or even a restaurant or warehouse. Individuals, corporations, and corporate interests may generate money from commercial real estate by leasing it out, or owning it and reselling it.

Commercial real estate comprises numerous categories, such as merchants of all kinds: office space, hotels and resorts, strip malls, restaurants, and healthcare facilities.

Commercial real estate refers to properties utilized exclusively for commercial or income-generating reasons. Commercial real estate varies from residential real estate since it can create profit for the property owner via capital gain or rental revenue.

The four primary types of commercial real estate are office space, industrial, multifamily rentals, and retail. Commercial real estate offers rental income as well as the possibility of some capital gain for investors.

Investing in commercial real estate typically demands greater skill and bigger quantities of cash from investors than does residential real estate.Publicly traded real estate investment trusts (REITs) are a realistic option for people to indirectly participate in commercial real estate.

The Basics of Commercial Real Estate

Commercial real estate and residential real estate are the two basic kinds of real estate property. Residential properties contain buildings intended for human residence and not for commercial or industrial usage. As its name indicates, commercial real estate is employed in commerce, and multiunit rental buildings that serve as dwellings for renters are considered a commercial activity for the landlord.

Commercial real estate is often classified into four groups, based on function:

1. Office space
2. Industrial usage
3. Multifamily rental
4. Retail

Individual categories may potentially be further categorized. There are, for instance, several various sorts of retail real estate:

1. Hotels and resorts
2. Strip malls

3. Restaurants
4. Healthcare facilities

Similarly, office space has various subcategories. It is typically categorized as class A, class B, or class C:

- Class A symbolizes the finest buildings in terms of beauty, age, quality of infrastructure, and location.
- Class B buildings are frequently older and not as competitive—price-wise—as class A buildings. Investors typically seek these structures for renovation.
- Class C buildings are the oldest, generally, more than 20 years of age, situated in less appealing regions, and in need of care.

Note that some zoning and licensing authorities further segregate off industrial properties sites used for the manufacturing and production of commodities, particularly heavy items—but most consider it a subset of commercial real estate.

Some companies own the premises that they inhabit. However, the more frequent arrangement is that the business property is leased. Usually, an investor or a group of investors controls the building and receives rent from each firm that runs there.

Commercial lease rates—the price to occupy a place for a defined period—are generally indicated in yearly rental dollars per square foot. Conversely, residential real estate rates quote as a yearly amount or a monthly rent.

Commercial leases may normally extend from one year to 10 years or more, with office and retail space often averaging five- to 10-year contracts. This might be contrasted with more short-term annual or month-to-month residential leases.

Research undertaken by real estate market analyst company CBRE Group revealed that the term—i.e., length—of a lease was related to the size of the space being rented. Further, the data suggested that renters would accept extended leases to lock in pricing in a growing market scenario. But it is not their sole motivating reason. Some tenants with the need for huge areas may accept extended leases owing to the restricted availability of property that suits their demands.

There are four major forms of commercial property leases, each demanding various degrees of obligation from the landlord and the tenant.

- A single net lease makes the renter liable for paying property taxes.
- A double net (NN) lease makes the renter accountable for paying property taxes and insurance.
- A triple net (NNN) lease makes the renter liable for paying property taxes, insurance, and upkeep.
- Under a gross lease, the tenant pays simply rent, while the landlord pays for the building's property taxes, insurance, and upkeep.

Owning and managing leased commercial real estate demands comprehensive and continuing supervision by the owner. Property owners may desire to engage a commercial real estate management business to assist them to discover, manage, and retain tenants, handling leases and financing alternatives, and coordinating property care and marketability. The specialist understanding of a commercial real estate management business is crucial since the laws and regulations regulating such property differ by state, county, municipality, industry, and size.

The landlord must typically find a compromise between boosting rents and limiting vacancies and tenant turnover. Turnover may be expensive for CRE owners since space must be altered to accommodate the individual demands of new tenants—for example, if a restaurant is moving into a building originally held by a yoga studio.

Commercial real estate (CRE) is an enticing investment sector because of its steady returns, passive income, and expansion potential. This area of real estate investing is growing more and more popular as an alternative investment. However, although CRE has the potential to be successful, not all commercial investments are regarded as equal. Knowing when, what, and how to invest in commercial real estate is a crucial component of success or failure.

Chapter 2

Investing in commercial real estate may be potentially rewarding and act as a hedge against the volatility of the stock market. Investors may earn money via property appreciation when they sell, but most profits come from tenant rentals.

Direct Investment

Investors may employ direct investments when they become landlords via the ownership of the actual property. People most suited for direct investment in commercial real estate are those that either has a great degree of expertise in the business or can engage companies that do. Commercial buildings are a high-risk, high-reward real estate investment. Such an investor is likely to be a high-net-worth person as CRE investment takes a large amount of money.

The ideal property is in a region with limited CRE supply and strong demand, which will yield favorable rental rates. The strength of the area's local economy also influences the value of the CRE acquisition.

Indirect Investment
Alternatively, investors may invest in the commercial market indirectly through either ownership of various market securities, such as real estate investment trusts (REITs) or exchange-traded funds (ETFs) that invest in commercial property-related stocks, or investment in companies that cater to the commercial real estate market, such as banks and Realtors.

Advantages of Commercial Real Estate
One of the main benefits of commercial real estate is competitive lease rates. In places where the quantity of new buildings is restricted by either land or regulation, commercial real estate may offer outstanding returns and large monthly cash flows. Industrial buildings often rent at a cheaper rate, yet they also have reduced

overhead expenditures compared with an office tower.

Commercial real estate also benefits from significantly longer lease arrangements with renters than residential real estate. This extended lease period affords commercial real estate owners a great level of cash flow stability, as long as long-term tenants inhabit the property.

In addition to giving a reliable and abundant source of income, commercial real estate provides the opportunity for capital growth, as long as the property is well-maintained and kept up to date. And, like other kinds of real estate, it is a separate asset class that may give an excellent diversification alternative to a balanced portfolio.

Disadvantages of Commercial Real Estate
Rules and regulations are the key deterrents for most persons intending to invest in commercial real estate directly. The taxes, mechanics of purchase, and upkeep duties for commercial

properties are hidden in layers of legalese. These criteria alter according to state, county, industry, size, zoning, and many more distinctions. Most investors in commercial real estate either have specific expertise or a payroll of people who do.

Another challenge is the increased risk presented with tenant turnover, particularly pertinent in an environment where unexpected retail closures leave buildings unoccupied with little prior warning.

With apartments, the facilities needs of one renter frequently match those of prior or prospective residents. However, with a commercial property, each renter may have quite diverse demands that necessitate significant remodeling. The property owner then needs to adjust the area to meet each tenant's particular trade. A business property with a low vacancy but significant tenant turnover may nonetheless lose money owing to the expense of upgrades for new tenants.

For individuals wishing to invest directly, purchasing a commercial property is a significantly more pricey proposition than a residential home. Moreover, although real estate in general is among the most illiquid of asset classes, deals for commercial buildings tend to move particularly slowly.

What is the difference between commercial and residential real estate?
Residential real estate is utilized solely for private dwelling quarters. Commercial real estate refers to any property utilized for commercial activity. Types of commercial real estate include hospitals, assembly factories, storage warehouses, retail complexes, office spaces, or any other place for a company organization.

Is commercial real estate a worthwhile investment?
It can be. Commercial real estate may generate remarkable returns and large monthly cash flows, and returns held up well throughout the

market shocks of the last decade. As with any investment, though, commercial real estate comes with hazards.

Commercial real estate (CRE) is an enticing investment sector because of its steady returns, passive income, and expansion potential. This area of real estate investing is growing more and more popular as an alternative investment. However, although CRE has the potential to be successful, not all commercial investments are regarded as equal. Knowing when, what, and how to invest in commercial real estate is a crucial component of success or failure.

If you want to invest in CRE, here are six things you need to know before you get started.

It's a crucial component to know the frequent dangers, blunders, and hazards of commercial real estate, so you can prepare for them before you acquire.

1. Not all property types are the same

Commercial real estate comprises a broad array of asset categories. While CRE is traditionally grouped into five broad sectors; industrial, office, retail, multifamily, and special purpose, there are numerous more property kinds such as self-storage, medical, elder care, land, or hotel. The supply and demand, yield, and overall profitability of each industry vary substantially.

Some property kinds do better than others depending on the supply and demand in the asset's unique area. But even on a macro level, certain industries do better than others. It is vital to know how to select the asset kinds that are most lucrative or give the best potential in the present economy.

Currently, industrial is the top-performing CRE asset type, while retail space is the lowest performing sector. With the increase of internet shopping, retail space is failing to compete, generating a shortage in returns and a reduction in growth. Keep in mind that certain sectors of commercial real estate tend to have higher vacancy rates since they may have a single tenant — like a warehouse in the industrial sector, or a single office space. To minimize the possible risk profile, some prefer to invest in industries or buildings that have many tenants such as multi-family flats.

Before you begin investing, analyze the performance of each asset class in the present economy, establish the feasibility of that sector as an investment, and then chose which CRE property type you would want to pursue.

2. Know the market area and supply and demand

One of the most crucial things to know before investing in commercial real estate is that every market is distinct. When you invest, you are investing in a specific geographic area that has its unique supply and demand. Certain property categories may be performing well on a global level yet you may discover there is an overstock in your city, or vice-versa. Oftentimes investors fail to undertake adequate market research to discover whether there is a possible danger of market saturation.

A smart place to start is investigating the market supply in your nearby region, taking into consideration both the present rentable square footage and any new square footage that will come from the current building and planned projects.

If you have discovered a property type that is undersupplied in your particular area, you may acquire a feasibility study to define the future growth and possibility of success in that sector.

3. Understand market cycles
Nothing lasts forever. The health of the economy, unemployment rate, and GDP are all closely linked to the profitability of commercial real estate. Understanding how real estate market cycles operate will help you avoid purchasing when the market is high and being forced to sell when the market is low. Additionally,

recognizing precise signs of the different market cycles can assist you to evaluate what possibilities are there right now and making better educated investing selections.

4. Do rigorous due diligence

The due diligence period is the time in which a potential buyer may undertake an extensive study on the investment possibility. This might involve evaluating financials, paperwork, tax returns, profit and loss statements from the previous owner, as well as completing surveys, property inspections, a feasibility study, or any other relevant research.

It's not unusual for rookie real estate investors to be so enthused about the possibility of purchasing their first commercial venture that they overlook anything in their due diligence. Having a strong knowledge of what has to be explored, thoroughly evaluated, and inspected before you buy can avoid you from possibly making extremely expensive errors.

Creating a detailed and broad due diligence checklist for your CRE property type can assist guarantee no issue gets neglected. Here are just a few typical things to consider:

- If you plan on developing unoccupied land, ensure that zoning will enable you to utilize the property as planned.
- If you wish to extend an existing building or develop a new one, examine to discover how many extra units a market can handle.
- Become acquainted with the permitting processes and expenses with the city or municipality of the property.
- If you are investing in more passive types of commercial real estate such as real estate investment trusts (REITs), crowdsourcing, partnerships, or private funds, your due diligence will entail properly verifying the organization or person who is administering your investment.

Unfortunately, not everyone in the financial sector follows the same set of rules. Due diligence on the person, fund manager, or organization you are investing with is just as vital as due diligence on the asset.

Speak with other participants that have invested in prior homes or ask for recommendations.
Look at prior offers and real returns on closed investments to get a sense of their track record.
Ask what their due diligence process is like. See how they evaluate each investment opportunity or choose which REIT or investment to participate in. While it may not be essential with large-scale investment business, if it's your first time dealing with someone in the private sector, complete a background check. While this may seem terrible, this is not unusual in bigger CRE purchases.

5. *Have a contingency and capital reserve money*
There is always unpredictability with every investment. Regardless matter how much you

studied, checked, or prepared, there will always be unknown elements that might favorably or adversely affect your total output. One strategy to hedge this uncertainty is to account for cost contingencies.

Cost contingencies are extra monies you put aside as a part of your original purchase costs to deal with unforeseen expenditures that develop when you lease up, increase rents, change management, remodel, rezone, or construct. They may also be utilized to assist fund your debt service until the property is stabilized. Cost contingencies are particularly beneficial if there will be negative cash flow while you enhance the property's overall performance. In commercial real estate, the normal contingency budget is 5%-15%, but may vary based on the asset and whether or not it is sub-performing.

Additionally, a recommended practice in real estate is to construct a capital reserve or replacement reserves fund. A capital reserve is a fund or account that has money put aside for long-term upgrades or unanticipated needs beyond your original capital improvements. This is money you put away before netting any positive income flow, often ranging from 3%-5% of gross rentals. Budgeting for both of these elements when you conduct your research of the investment will assist raise the odds of being successful and having the cash accessible should unforeseen circumstances happen.

6. Be prepared for setbacks and prolonged timetables

Just as there is uncertainty with expenses, there are also uncertainties with the timetable. Most individuals establish unrealistic timetables in which to develop, refurbish, completely lease, or attain market rents for their CRE venture. New construction, renovations, rising rents, changing management, and implementing new systems all require time. There will virtually always be setbacks and hurdles that hinder growth. Try to identify the probable hurdles in your due diligence phase and prepare for them as a part of your contingency expenses or with a plan of action that may be executed if delays develop.

If you are investing in commercial real estate via a more passive vehicle like a REIT, crowdsourcing, partnership, or fund, be sure you are flexible in your return expectations and timescales. Asset performances might change due to economic conditions, market cycles, or issues that develop after the purchase. The fund manager ultimately must appropriately notify you of this risk, but it's also smart to be cognizant of it on your own.

Chapter 3

Commercial Real Estate has traditionally been a strong and reasonably steady investment vehicle for people wishing to maintain their wealth while developing their portfolios. As the number of investors seeking direct co-investment into real estate continues to expand, so does the possibility to distribute money on a deal-by-deal basis. Add this to a consistently improving economy, interest rates continuing at historical lows, and commercial lenders prepared to do everything it takes to gain borrowers' business - there is no better time than NOW to invest in Commercial Real Estate.

However, we'd be negligent if we didn't note that we are in the tenth year of the longest economic boom in US history with a recession seeming approaching. The bottom has to come out at some time. Some industry experts go so far as to claim if you haven't already invested in commercial real estate, you've missed the boat, while others feel there are "recession resistant" opportunities still available. In truth, it's simply a question of being wise about the assets you select.

When "those in the know" are adopting such dramatically opposing perspectives on the status of the commercial real estate market, it leaves investors with a dilemma of what to do. Here's the good news - whether you're pessimistic and think we're due for a slowdown, or a bull and feel this economy will continue to have legs, NOW is a wonderful moment to invest in commercial real estate.

Here are five reasons why:

1) Increased Demand for Office Space
With unemployment at 3.6% (the lowest it's been since 1969), a mature millennial population approaching its peak earning years, and corporate giants becoming bigger, the desire for additional square footage is evident. Look no further than the current Fortune 500 list. Some time ago, America's 500 biggest corporations

hauled in $13.7 trillion in sales — more than two-thirds of the whole US economy. As firms continue to develop, their need for commercial real estate to house their enterprises will also increase.

2) Ongoing Cash Flow

One of the most essential advantages of commercial real estate is the cash flow produced by rentals. Secured by leases, commercial real estate investments may generate constant, passive income; revenue that comes in independent of the market cycle.

3) Hedging Against Inflation

During periods of increasing inflation, clever investors may strive to hedge against it by investing in commercial real estate. Commercial property valuations are generally based on operating income and market capitalization rates. In general, when inflation happens, rents increase. This rise leads to an increase in operational revenue, which ultimately increases property prices. As you can see, this connection permits commercial real estate to act as a significant hedge against inflation.

4) *Low Volatility*

Simply stated, many investors may pick commercial real estate investments because they are physical assets with intrinsic worth. What's more, the low volatility of direct investments in commercial real estate might help to counterbalance other, more volatile assets in your portfolio. The counter-cyclical characteristics of commercial real estate, along with minimal correlation to other asset classes (when invested directly), may operate as a defensive position during times of economic slowdown. Over the long run, the value of real property in the US – including commercial buildings – has constantly gone increased.

5) *Appreciation Potential*

Under the correct ownership, commercial assets are likely to rise in value. This means that there is potential to reap further gains when an asset is sold.

Commercial real estate gives investors predictable cash flow, appreciation benefits, and large tax advantages when compared to other popular asset types.

It relies on the kind of your company and how fast your business revenue will be able to recover the acquisition expenditures of the property. But on average, experts believe that owning commercial buildings is a fantastic decision for company owners for a handful of reasons.

Reasons why it makes sense to own your company premises as opposed to renting it
While most individuals who plan and invest in their retirement portfolio often do so by investing in the stock market, investing in commercial real estate may be rewarding too.

Besides, we are all aware that stock market investments are very variable and it's hard to be certain of secure returns. Instead of placing all eggs in one basket, it's always a smart approach to diversify your assets.

Retirement savings might be an excellent source of money while you begin your commercial real estate investment. And as the initial stage, it's a terrific idea to acquire the property you intend to house your firm. If you're operating a company already, that's plus one incentive for you to acquire the property.

You may not be positive about how long your firm will continue, but as a matter of fact, nobody is. Buying it is still secure as you can always sell the home at much greater resale prices at a later date if things don't work out in your favor.

If not anything, even in the worst-case scenario – you will recover more than what you invest today after a period of 3 to 4 years because, unlike stock markets, real estate markets are less fluctuating and they generally always appreciate (unless there's a real boom in the country's economy to the extent that the real estate markets will crash to ground which however is highly unlikely).

You may leverage the advantages granted to owners on their owner-occupied homes under various lending schemes. Different lending programs under the USA Small Company Administration give varying benefits to business owners who own their properties. In other words, as a business person, you might have several advantages by only electing to acquire the property in which you conduct your firm.

The most interesting part here which most people ignore is the clauses that specify that you don't need to completely function in the company space that you wish to acquire.

You are needed merely to operate your company activities, covering 51% of the territory, and are always at liberty to rent out the other 49%.

What does this imply to you as an owner? You may own your property and also generate a nice rental income on the areas of the property that you do not use for your company, yet have complete ownership over the building and enjoy all the advantages afforded by SBA lending programs. That's good news.

And as an owner, if and when your firm does develop, and you discover a need to extend your area of operation, you are always at liberty to utilize the remainder of the building when the lease or rent period of your renters finishes. So, that's a win-win for both scenarios.

You may fully reduce your monthly leasing overheads. You don't have to pay rent to your landlord when you buy the commercial premises you run your company.

A clear no-brainer, right? Although it may seem like a no-brainer, it is remarkable how most individuals do not think about it at all and continue to keep paying rentals for their company premises even after a long time of 10 to 15 years has gone.

Ask any small business owner about the number of years they're in the same business at the same location and how much they have paid as rent on their property. The answers could catch you by surprise. More frequently than not, you'll see that these owners have ended up paying more than the property worth itself in the long run, without even recognizing it.

They could have purchased the home in half the sum they've expended as a rental charge throughout the years. If you do not want yourself to remain in a location like that, after a few years – you might consider owning your business property.

Instead of just paying a big amount of your company profits as rent, you'll be producing wealth for yourself if you opt to pay the same on acquiring your home.

And how do you do that? By getting commercial real estate loans that'll span beyond a few years.

After completion of the loan time, you become the owner of the land, and you have something to call "yours."

Bottom-line: Instead of making your landlord more productive by paying rent on your property when you know you're going to stay in the same company line for some years, acquire it and put this expenditure towards producing wealth for yourself.

Commercial real estate lending rates have unexpectedly been cheap! Unless you already have a lot of money to acquire your property with a single huge down payment, you're going to have to seek a suitable Commercial real estate loan.

And unexpectedly, and a pleasant one at that - the Commercial real estate lending rates are cheap! Very low. Residential loan rates are normally three times higher than commercial loan rates.

These cheap prices make it much simpler for you to pick and go forward with owning the home than renting it. And from the last several years, this year has been one of those years with jaw-dropping loan rates.

So, you don't have to worry about the "extra" charges you'll be spending to acquire your house since there have never been rates as cheap as it is today!

You may rent your commercial space to the successor of your company! The last important argument as to why you should acquire the place you conduct your company in is – you may rent it out to the successor of your firm.

Employees retire, and individuals in business need to quit working actively too, at a point in time. And when your time comes, and you have located a suitable successor for your firm, you don't have to sell your property too along with your business.

Instead, you may rent the facility out to your successor, and that creates a different revenue source for you entirely. How's that for a smart retirement plan? You may then rest back throughout your old age while your financial requirements will be taken care of by this business property you own.

Bottom line: Owning your commercial property is a win-win right from the start, up to the moment you choose to quit working actively in your firm.

Chapter 4

Investing in real estate is a terrific method to acquire money. Commercial real estate investment, in particular, is renowned to produce some of the largest revenue streams. If you've been investing in residential real estate for a few years and have been wondering how to invest in commercial real estate, this article helps to break down everything you need to know to get started.

Offices, hotels, retail establishments, and other commercial real estate investments have suffered substantially during the COVID-19 epidemic. While the epidemic isn't over yet, commercial real estate is likely to continue a pattern of economic recovery in the year ahead. Many commercial real estate investors are bullish as the sector continues to adjust to changes.

While the start of 2021 did not guarantee a favorable picture, analysts indicated commercial real estate will stabilize towards the end of the year. According to Kathy Feucht, global real estate head at Deloitte, commercial real estate investors aimed to decrease expenses by roughly 25% in 2021. However, there were numerous shocks during the recent year, notably higher demand for industrial buildings.

Julian Goldie, CEO of Goldie Agency, argues that "given the opportunity for outsized gains, steady yields, volatility hedges, and unique tax perks, more quants are anticipated to join the market this year. Tailwinds are blowing throughout the market as a consequence of the post-Covid bounce and infrastructure expenditure, and astute investors should pay attention".

With that in mind, there are numerous forecasted trends for 2022 based on the sort of commercial real estate investment. Let's look at how these different attributes are predicted to perform:

Retail Stores: Several retail departments went bankrupt in 2020 and 2021 as the economy responded to quarantines and high COVID-19 transmission rates. As more and more individuals purchase online, analysts expect up to 25% fewer retail outlets by 2025. Retail establishments in metropolitan regions, including New York and San Francisco, are likely to be replaced by healthcare, food, and other alternative outlets.

Offices: According to CBRE, office demand might be permanently decreased by 15% as more firms transition to work-from-home practices. As a consequence, the office building supply will continue to expand. However, we have witnessed the growth of "hybrid" office rules during the past year, forcing employees to come in just on specific days of the week. This tendency may stabilize office spaces as firms explore methods to keep some in-person workdays.

Hotels: Hotels are anticipated to suffer throughout the year ahead, despite some easing limitations on tourism. Many are not anticipated to recover until 2023, while expensive hotels that provide amenities for guests won't stabilize until 2025. Hotels in more populous cities will suffer the most as many attempts to steer clear of heavily congested regions.

Warehouses: Warehouses are predicted to be the top performance among commercial real estate investments. Their success is attributable to enterprises striving to keep up with the increased demand for e-commerce orders. Real estate analysts estimated an extra need of 250 million square feet for warehouse space in 2021.

Apartments: Initially, apartments were predicted to suffer during the epidemic since many would be unable to pay rent. However, multifamily complexes are operating well since the need for housing has not been reduced. With flats at more affordable costs and historically low-interest rates, they are projected to stay steady in the year ahead.

Rental Property Upgrades: Multifamily property owners may see an upsurge in applications for bigger apartments as tenants adjust to work-from-home lifestyles. Upgraded flats may also become more popular in competitive areas throughout 2022 as tenants strive to enhance their living circumstances.

Commercial Development: New development projects are likely to expand as housing markets throughout the nation struggle to fulfill rising needs for homes. Commercial investors proficient in development projects may find many prospects for new developments in the year ahead.

Commercial real estate is a property that is often leased out for commercial and retail uses. Investing in commercial real estate entails the acquisition or construction of facilities that have been developed to accommodate business tenants. Unlike a residential real estate investor, commercial real estate investors lease out and collect rent from the companies that use their premises rather than from residential tenants. It should also be emphasized that raw land acquired for commercial property projects is also included in this definition.

Owner-occupied commercial real estate (OOCRE) is when investors acquire commercial real estate to use the building for their purposes. This method may be used in any of the five commercial real estate categories outlined above.

The chance to inhabit the business real estate you invest in is only one of the numerous perks of commercial investment. Keep reading to discover some of the additional perks that may spark your curiosity. Investing in commercial real estate may be highly rewarding, both emotionally and financially. For many, the purpose of investing in commercial real estate is for future riches and stability; others employ it for tax advantages and investment portfolio diversification.

A commercial redeveloper may also make use of the following benefits:

Larger Income: The hallmark advantage of investing in commercial real estate is a higher prospective income. Generally speaking, commercial properties offer a superior return on investment, an average of six to twelve percent, whereas single-family buildings fetch between one and four percent. Secondly, commercial real estate gives a smaller vacancy risk, since buildings tend to have more available units.

(Consider this: one vacancy in an office building with 25 commercial spaces will adversely affect an investor's bottom line more than one vacancy in a residential duplex.) Also, business leases are often lengthier than those you would find in residential real estate. This implies that commercial real estate owners have to cope with significantly less tenant churn.

Cash Flow: Commercial real estate has one very obvious advantage: a generally continuous source of revenue owing to longer lease durations. In addition, commercial buildings frequently have more units than residential properties, which means you may achieve economies of scale and expand your revenue streams much more rapidly. Known in the industry as a triple net lease, many commercial tenants additionally pay the building's real estate taxes, property insurance, and maintenance expenses, thereby enhancing your owner's advantages.

Less Competition: Another benefit connected with commercial real estate is generally less competition. Because of the perceived difficulties of commercial investment, the commercial area tends to be less flooded with other investors.

Longer Leases: Perhaps one of the major rewards of commercial real estate is the lucrative lease terms. Commercial buildings often have lengthier lease terms with tenants compared to residential properties, which, as previously said, provide investors with remarkable returns and a large monthly cash flow. In many circumstances, leasing agreements for commercial premises are negotiated for numerous years.

Business Interactions: The world of commercial real estate gives investors the unique chance to engage in business-to-business relationships. This may lead to more professional, neighborly relationships with your renters as compared to residential real estate. In certain circumstances, you may even be able to create connections with the company owners renting in your building. This may be wonderful for building your network and becoming active in the community you are investing in.

Limited Operational Hours: One of the lesser-known positives of running commercial real estate is that, for the most part, you share working hours with your tenants. While business hours might vary significantly, commercial property owners normally won't find themselves addressing around-the-clock maintenance requests or other tenants' contacts. On the other hand, residential real estate might need an on-call staff person to deal with difficulties 24/7. Many commercial investors who prefer to manage their properties appreciate this advantage, as it helps allow for a feeling of separation between property ownership and ordinary life.

Commercial real estate investing gives investors an assortment of options and benefits that other investment techniques do not. Once the advantages of commercial real estate investment are acknowledged, the next step is to plunge in.

The topic of 'how to invest in commercial real estate has just one answer: due diligence. Regardless of what industry or specialty you're in, conducting your study and performing your due diligence is vital in ensuring your success in real estate. Besides understanding the ins and outs of commercial investment, make sure you grasp the commercial real estate market and how it might vary from the residential real estate industry. If you're ready to begin on your first commercial enterprise, be sure to adhere to the following tips:

1. Understand How Commercial Real Estate Is Different
The first step as a business investor is recognizing that commercial real estate is priced differently than residential properties. Unlike residential real estate, the revenue from commercial real estate is often proportional to usable square footage. Also, commercial property leases often continue longer than residential leases. These two criteria explain why a commercial real estate investor has a stronger chance to make a bigger income.

Matt Woodley from Mover Focus suggests "start by conducting your homework. Make sure you understand the risks and advantages of commercial real estate investment. Also, be prepared to commit a considerable amount of money initially, and be ready to weather some bad market conditions".

Location is a vital element regardless of your investment specialization, with commercial investing being no exception. However, commercial investors also need to pay particular attention to their tenant type. The location and desired tenant type are two criteria that overlap closely when determining demand. For example, a facility built for corporate offices would typically function better in an urban center than in a predominantly residential zone. Analyzing current comparables might offer you a clearer sense of how your property of interest could fare.

2. Analyze Comparables

The next stage is to study comparables in the region and explore potential developments. Otherwise known as "comps," these assets relate to prices paid for previously sold homes that are comparable in location, size, and style. Analyzing comps can help you identify the current market value of a property. When choosing comps, a typical rule of thumb is to pick a home where the square footage does not go above 10 percent greater or lower than that of the property being analyzed. This will enable the most precise comparison possible.

3. Use The Right Success Metric

Commercial real estate investment needs a broad variety of computations and a mastery of real estate financing. To be a participant in commercial real estate, there are various formulae you need to know.

Net Operating Income: This is a figure that equals all income and expenses from a single property. Configured before taxes, this number offers investors an indication of how much they'll receive from an investment without any essential running expenditures. Operating expenditures often consist of insurance, property management fees, utilities, repairs, cleaning fees, and property tax.

Cap Rate: Used to evaluate the worth of income-producing assets, the "cap rate" — short for capitalization rate — will offer investors an estimate of future earnings or cash flow. This is effectively the ratio of net operating income to the property asset value.

Cash On Cash: Cash on cash is a measure that offers investors a rate of return on their commercial real estate deals. It's frequently employed by investors who depend on loans to acquire their homes. Cash on cash evaluates the return on out-of-pocket cash invested compared to the part that was financed. This will offer an accurate appraisal of an investment's performance.

4. Reserve Cost Contingencies

Cost contingencies are rainy-day reserves that are put aside to meet unforeseen acquisition costs. This component of your budget might be utilized to compensate for missed income flow due to early vacancies, renovations, and other upfront charges. For example, the property may need to be rezoned or you may need to engage new property management. These expenditures might sometimes be incurred before you have reliable cash flow.

By integrating cost contingencies into your budget early on, you can guarantee you have the means to make up for unexpected expenditures. A common cost contingency budget in commercial investment is between 5 and 15 percent. To establish the proper figure for your investment, assess your projected cash flow in the first few months. Will that figure cover early loan expenses? What about alterations to the property? Even if you anticipate cash flow to be sustainable early on, it is always a good idea to have additional money just in case.

In addition to cost contingencies, many investors may put aside a capital reserves fund which effectively serves the same function later on. These funds may be utilized for unforeseen costs and are integrated into the operational budget. Overall, by preparing for these fees throughout the investing process you may prevent circumstances when you are tight on cash. When it comes to commercial investment, cost contingencies and cash reserves are significant components of the process.

5. Commercial Real Estate Investing Mistakes To Avoid

As a commercial real estate investor, it's just as vital to know what not to do as it is to know what to do. Today's finest investors already know it, and it's about time you knew too: minimizing risk is the single greatest thing a real estate entrepreneur can do for the success of their firm. Mitigating risk exposure is the greatest method to maximize the chance of success. That said, here's a list of some of the most frequent errors commercial real estate investors need to avoid:

Improper Valuations: Every single commercial property is unique, and investors need to be able to account for differences that may be discovered in each asset. Failure to account for every aspect involved in an asset's appraisal might lead to financial devastation. Therefore, commercial real estate investors must be well informed of what they are purchasing and for how much. The failure to account for the full worth of a property will affect practically every step going forward, so it's crucial to get things right from the moment of purchase.

Financial Ignorance: Failing to comprehend the financial aspects of commercial real estate investment may be fatal. IF for nothing else, commercial agreements are not the same as residential ones. Investors will need to understand the distinctions, not the least of which include the loan-to-value (LTV) or debt service coverage ratio (DSCR) (DSCR).

Neglecting Due Diligence: While today's market necessitates decisive decision-making, it's crucial to remember due diligence. It's better to lose a contract to someone else than to buy into a deal you aren't prepared for. As a consequence, more investors need to spend the right time to study as much about a property as they can before they acquire it.

Not Working With a Team: Far too many investors desire to save money by doing everything alone. However, working as a team is superior to working alone. While you may seem to save money on the surface, chances are you are wasting both money and time by working alone. That stated, match your services with professional staff and trust them to accomplish the task you hired them for. There's a high possibility they know more about every procedure than you do.

Now that you've gotten an introduction to commercial real estate investing, including its advantages and suggestions on how to get started, you'll need to start thinking about a key aspect: How will you go about financing these investments?

There is a vast selection of commercial investment loan kinds, and it is up to the investor to pick which financing option best meets their requirements. Each form of loan has distinct qualifying conditions, such as a minimum credit score, experience level, and down payment need. These loans also have varied parameters, including the loan period, interest rate, and loan-to-value (LTV) ratio. For example, one investor may be in quest of a loan that provides lower interest rates over a longer loan period, while another investor's focus would be seeking a short-term loan as a method of bridging a financial gap.

The prospect of acquiring commercial real estate finance may seem frightening at first. Still, investors who learn about the procedure and the numerous forms of commercial real estate loans will discover that they are fully reachable. Below are the basic stages required in acquiring a business investment property loan:

Individual Vs Entity: Step one is to select whether to finance a commercial property as an individual or as an entity. Although most commercial real estate is acquired by corporate organizations such as companies, developers, and business partnerships, it may simply be performed by an individual investor. The lender generally wants to be certain the borrower can return the loan, therefore asking borrowers to submit financial track records to receive a loan. The lender will normally need the investor(s) to guarantee the loan for younger enterprises with no credit history.

Mortgage Options: Investors must know that residential and business mortgages are not the same. First, unlike residential mortgages, business loans are not guaranteed by government entities such as Freddie Mac and Fannie Mae. Secondly, commercial loan conditions vary from those of residential buildings. Commercial loans vary from five to 20 years, and residential loans normally range from 15 to 30 years. Lenders will normally make their selections based on an investor's financial and credit background.

Loan To Value Ratio: An essential measure lenders assess when financing commercial real estate is a property's loan-to-value ratio (LTV) (LTV). This number reflects the value of a loan versus the value of the property. It is computed by dividing the loan amount by the property's appraisal value or purchase price. The LTV will range from 65 to 80 percent for commercial loans, with lower LTVs qualifying for more advantageous financing rates.

Debt Service Coverage Ratio: Lenders often look at the debt-service coverage ratio (DSCR) (DSCR). This indicator gauges a property's capacity to pay the debt. It compares a property's yearly net operational revenue to its annual mortgage debt payment, including principal and interest. A DSCR of less than one percent implies a negative cash flow. Commercial lenders normally aim for DSCRs of at least 1.25 to guarantee appropriate cash flow.

Once you've acquired your finance, you are ready to start exploring through listings. However, there is a lot of information to digest at once.

A successful commercial real estate investor has the potential to have a highly prosperous career. Many rookie investors utilize multifamily buildings as a bridge to enter into commercial real estate investment. Regardless, you must have a comprehensive business strategy before getting started.

The following three questions were meant to assist you to acquire greater clarity on whether or not commercial real estate is for you:

Do you have the capacity to think big?
Investing in commercial real estate needs folks to dream large and have an open mind. When investing in residential real estate, the properties under consideration are substantially smaller in size. With a commercial property, you must

envisage a final result even at the earliest phases of redevelopment. If you are deciding whether to acquire a five-unit apartment or a property with ten or more units, it is generally more profitable to pick the 10. If the five-unit complex needs almost the same commercial financing as the 10, it makes sense to dream large and do what it takes to enhance your bottom line.

Are you an exceptional connection builder?
Networking and creating contacts as a residential real estate investor are vital, but it is an absolute requirement for commercial investors. The primary incentive to create ties with other commercial investors and private lenders is for financial needs. When confronting a one million dollars or more buying price, you will likely require finance. What better approach to get cash than to call one of your private lenders with whom you've already formed a connection? Once you've developed a network, you can depend on other folks who have made and learned from their errors.

Can you effectively complete your due diligence?

Arguably the most critical duty rookie investors can do before going into commercial real estate investment is to do their due research. After you've picked your expertise, you must investigate all you can about that particular area. Ask inquiries from like-minded folks at your local REI club, discover information about various sorts of financing alternatives online, and reach out to private lenders in advance. Hence, you know precisely what facts to give them when the time comes. Once you've carried out extensive due diligence, you will be ready to effectively begin your first commercial real estate purchase.

You do not need a real estate license to begin investing in commercial real estate, however, it may open opportunities professionally. Obtaining your real estate license and handling deals on the side might help you create professional relationships within the sector – and make money via commission in the interim. For many investors, these monies may go immediately into acquiring commercial buildings and increasing their portfolios.

That being said, there are training hours, tests, and more that are necessary to earn a real estate license. It will take a time commitment to even start practicing as an agent, which might be tough if you are already beginning to grow your investment portfolio. Some investors may prefer to develop a network of real estate agents rather than get their license.

Commercial real estate investment may appear frightening at first, but you should recognize that the essential skills and competencies necessary are the same as residential property investing. They involve performing due diligence, having a suitable company strategy that includes knowing finance sources, and creating a strong network. Any sort of investment is connected with some amount of risk, and it's up to you to discover strategies to manage that risk. If you apply the techniques that gave you success with residential real estate and smoothly incorporate them into your business plan, you will undoubtedly discover success.

www.ingramcontent.com/pod-product-compliance
Lightning Source LLC
Chambersburg PA
CBHW070318220526
45465CB00004B/1894